I was born in Walth
1963. As a young gir
to Spain to start a ne
brother and two sisters. I thoroughly
enjoyed my younger years growing up
and schooling in a different country.We
eventually moved back to the UK living in
Marlow, Buckinghamshire.
I had a son in 1989 but it wasn't until I
met my now husband in 2008. I moved to
Essex to live with him and we married in
2012 extending my now family to 3
children and lovely grandchildren.
It was 2015 aged 52 that I was diagnosed
with this awful and somewhat unknown
autoimmune illness that only affects 1 in
100.000 people. I have written this book
in dedication and to help raise awareness
for Achalasia..

I would like to acknowledge and give credit to "KELLY RENSHAW" a fellow Achalasian, who allowed me to use her amazing drawing for my front book cover, a drawing which needs no words to express how it feels to have Achalasia and how it affects us!
A very talented artist goes without saying and I cannot thank this young lady enough for allowing me to use her drawing...

Kelly Renshaw

@Kellysachalasiastory

I would like to thank the Professors, doctors, surgeons, nurses and caring staff at Queens Hospital, Romford.
Homerton Hospital, Hackney.
University College London Hospital for all your help and care over the last 6 years.
My husband John for always being there.
My family and friends for their love and support..

LIVING WITH 'A'

Well I really don't know where to start?
But my story begins back in late 2014
early 2015..
I'm not sure exactly when the signs
began, but my furthest memory goes
back to the end of 2014 when the
symptoms that I was having are now what
I know are the classic signs of
'A'(ACHALASIA)... which I can only
describe as the cruelest of illnesses!!!

ACHALASIA IS A SERIOUS AUTOIMMUNE
CONDITION THAT AFFECTS YOUR
ESOPHAGUS

The lower esophageal sphincter (LES) is a muscular ring that closes off the esophagus to the stomach. If you have Achalasia, your LES fails to open up during swallowing, which it's supposed to do. This leads to a backup of food within your esophagus"
This is a rare condition that only affects 1 in 100.000 people.

Achalasia is a rare disorder of the food pipe (oesophagus), which can make it difficult to swallow food and drink.

Normally, the muscles of the oesophagus contract to squeeze food along towards the stomach. A ring of muscle at the end of the food pipe then relaxes to let food into the stomach.

In achalasia, the muscles in the oesophagus don't contract correctly and the ring of muscle can fail to open properly, or doesn't open at all. Food and drink cannot pass into the stomach and becomes stuck. It is often brought back up.

Symptoms of achalasia

Not everyone with achalasia will have symptoms.

But most people with achalasia will find it difficult to swallow food or drink (known as dysphagia). Swallowing tends to get gradually more difficult or painful over a couple of years, to the point where it is sometimes impossible.

Other symptoms include:

- bringing back up undigested food
- choking and coughing fits
- heartburn
- chest pain
- repeated chest infections
- drooling of vomit or saliva
- gradual but significant weight loss

Symptoms of achalasia may start at any time of life.

Long-term untreated achalasia very slightly increases the risk of developing <u>cancer of the oesophagus</u>. This means it is important to get appropriate treatment for achalasia straight away, even if your symptoms are not bothering you.

Causes of achalasia

Achalasia is thought to happen when the nerves in the oesophagus become damaged and stop working properly, which is why the muscles and ring of muscle don't work. The exact cause of this is unknown.

I remember eating my dinner thinking it was just me rushing my food? It would all suddenly back up and felt as though I was going to choke! I would quickly rush to the toilet and regurgitate all of my food..My next memory is waking up in the middle of the night choking thinking I was going to be sick, bringing food up left in my esophagus. Another was constant reflux and burning in my chest to the point that it would make me sick and light headed.

Now that I've been diagnosed with 'A' I'm aware of all the early signs, which include all of the above.

The symptoms gradually worsened especially the reflux. My husband urged me to go to my GP for some tests.

2015 began much the same as any other year. My GP referred me to a Gastrologist at my local hospital, where he referred me to have some tests done at the 'Royal London Hospital'. The test I had to endure is called a 'Manometry' which I can hand on heart only describe as an awful test which I would NOT wish on anyone.

Esophageal Manometry is an outpatient test used to identify problems with the movement and pressure in the Esophagus that may lead to problems like heartburn and reflux.
The esophagus is the 'food pipe' leading from the mouth to the stomach.
Manometry measures the strength and muscle coordination of your esophagus when you swallow.

When we returned to see the Gastrologist for my results with my husband, he confirmed that I had Achalasia, what was

Achalasia? We did not have a clue, we had never heard of this?
He said he would refer me to Queens Hospital to see a specialist he knows of that has dealt with cases of 'Achalasia'. After a couple of months in March 2015 I got my referral to see Mr 'A' at Queens Hospital in Romford after having an Endoscopy, I received the diagnosis that I had 'ACHALASIA'!

Sadly it all coincided with my late mother's diagnosis with 'Esophageal' cancer. This can coincidentally mirror similar symptoms to Achalasia so naturally my immediate thought as well as Achalasia is that I may have cancer? Whilst having some ongoing appointments with Mr 'A' my poor mum was undergoing surgery (Esophagectomy) to remove the tumour in Oxford over 70 miles away from me!
Things didn't go well. My mum got an infection and ended up being put into an

induced coma to help her recover.
We actually thought we would lose mum there and then. Every weekend my husband took me to Oxford to visit my mum. Without my husband's love and support at this very tough time I don't know how I would have coped with my health and the constant worry of my mum. My mum being a tough lady pulled through after nearly 3 months in hospital to have her birthday at home with her family in June.

My symptoms progressively worsened. I was hardly eating, losing weight and feeling at my lowest.

I was finally scheduled for my 1st surgical procedure (Hellers Myotomy) with Dor Fundoplication. This was to be performed in November 2015.

Laparoscopic Heller Myotomy

Laparoscopic Heller myotomy is a **minimally invasive** procedure that opens the tight lower esophageal sphincter (the valve between the esophagus and the stomach) by performing a myotomy (cutting the thick muscle of the lower part of the esophagus and the upper part of the stomach) to relieve the **dysphagia** (difficulty swallowing). Further, a Dor fundoplication (a partial wrapping of the stomach around the esophagus to make a low-pressure valve) is performed to prevent reflux from the stomach into the esophagus following the myotomy. There is a very small chance that patients may develop reflux despite Dor fundoplication and may need to be treated with antacid medication.

Sadly we lost our mum in August of 2015 to Esophageal cancer, a very very sad time, especially at a time that I needed my mum. My husband is my tower of strength.

I could not go through what I'm going through in my life without him.

Not long after I started to get regular panic attacks, some worse than others. The main ones I remember was we were babysitting and for no reason suddenly I couldn't breath. I thought I was going to pass out.. It escalated. My husband called for an ambulance and I was rushed to Southend hospital. Where the doctor asks if I have any underlying problems? I said I suffer from Achalasia and he said what's that! It was the Junior doctor that had heard of it and had to explain to the doctor what it was..

I had tests and again I was dehydrated and lacking vitamins from lack of food. The next one which for me was the scariest I was asleep and suddenly woke up in a state of panic and not being able to breath or even move! My husband was beside himself. He called 999 and the paramedics arrived, this time a lovely lady calmed me down and spoke to me about the attacks. She showed me ways to calm me down and believed this was linked to the stresses in my life and having recently lost my mother had just tipped me over the edge!

In November 2015 my surgery was performed and things went to plan.
I stayed overnight for observation. The next day late afternoon I was allowed to go home, beforehand I was visited on the ward by Mr 'A' . He was so sure that my surgery was a success that he insisted that I try to eat a sandwich!!

Shock horror bread, for me this had been forbidden food because of my 'A' for fear of it getting stuck! I did what he asked, it was a struggle and very frightening and for me felt way too early to try something like this? Let me explain why. With 'A' all your muscles in your esophagus and lower sphincter stop functioning so all foods have to literally be forced down by gravity and with fluids to help them get to your stomach. This is for myself a very slow process and sometimes very painful, uncomfortable and traumatic...

We headed home, after waiting hours for my prescription of painkillers to take home with me, which were very much needed. On the way home I started getting severe pain and breathlessness, my breathing was very laboured. My husband, being very concerned, immediately turned the car around and headed back to the hospital. I remember the journey back very well, sheer panic and worry by myself and husband were thinking allsorts of things had happened. We arrived at A&E and by now I could hardly breathe. I really thought this was it and I was going to have a heart attack. My husband demanded immediate attention out of sheer panic. I was taken immediately into a cubicle where Mr 'A's registrar attended me. I was kept in a cubicle, where I was kept overnight for further observation and tests. It came to light that I had a lesion on my liver which I had sustained during my procedure, which caused my breathing problems. I also had calcium deficiency and was put on a drip. I was assured it would heal in time, the next morning I went home. My first HM was eventful to say the least.. And so begins my journey with 'A' again!

My recovery went fairly well, my wounds healed. I was managing some soft foods, nothing too much. After 6-8 weeks I had the horrible feeling back again, that food was sticking and not going down into my stomach! To be honest I knew in my heart of hearts it was going back to just how it was before my procedure.

I had my follow up appointment at Queens with my surgeon a few weeks later, where I explained in detail what was beginning to happen again.. He was actually very upset as he had been so confident this would work, myself and my husband were devastated to say the least after everything all we wanted was to get my life back again and just be normal!! He decided that he would try balloon dilation..

Balloon Dilation

In achalasia, disrupting the spastic muscle at the end of the esophagus (lower esophageal sphincter) can be done by using a balloon dilator. The achalasia balloon dilators are usually larger in diameter than regular dilators, starting at 30 millimeters (1.18 inches). They are positioned to overlay the hypertrophied lower esophageal sphincter and are then inflated to a preset size. A successful procedure leaves a controlled tear in the layers of the lower esophageal sphincter. The process will be repeated if necessary and the size of the balloon can be increased every time to reach satisfactory results.

The achalasia balloon dilation is done under direct visualization by X-ray (fluoroscopy). Endoscopic pneumatic dilation of the lower esophageal sphincter is the most effective nonsurgical treatment for achalasia. It is a generally safe procedure; the risk of esophageal perforation after balloon dilation was described in only 1.6 percent of the cases.

I had the dilation in March 2016. This is done as a day procedure so I went home the same day with my husband all fingers crossed! I was sore for a couple of days which is perfectly normal. Within the space of 1 to 2 weeks it was no better and things gradually worsened again.. I had another consultation with Mr 'A' and he decided on a 2nd dilation although reluctant because the more its stretched the weaker your esophagus becomes which can lead to complications.

My 2nd dilation was scheduled for April 2016. It was done and sadly this was also unsuccessful. We were beside ourselves as to where this was going to go? What next? Mr 'A' was unsure how to proceed. He had done all he was able to do with his expertise. He decided to refer me to a specialist of Achalasia at Homerton Hospital in Hackney,London...

This was the start of me feeling like I was being passed from one to the other because they had no idea what to do with me, it was as if he'd washed his hands of me to give me to someone else to deal with, we were devastated..

Achalasia is such a rare illness, which is incurable. There is no known cause for Achalasia even my own GP had no idea what it was!

And so it went on. I had my consultation with my new gastro consultant Mr 'B' at Homerton Hospital. After a long consultation a lot of questions from myself and my husband. His decision was to do a redo fundoplication.. Basically this means the previous operation is taken down (undone) and then they redo the previous surgery procedure again trying to keep the opening to my stomach from closing.

This can have many complications as does any other repeat surgery.

What choice do I have now? Continue to struggle or put my faith again into the medical profession..I cannot carry on like this.

So my 2nd keyhole surgery was schedule for the end of June 2016

Achalasia is a hidden autoimmune illness, I guess if you didn't know me to look at me you wouldn't think there is anything medically wrong with me, but 'A' is cruel it chips away at you mentally and physically day by day.
I used to be a healthy person before being diagnosed with this awful illness. I was a regular runner.

I ran the London marathon in sub: 4.30 hours, I ran many half marathons, and loved being active. Once 'A' got its grip my energy levels depleted, my stamina was zero and all my muscles deteriorated!

I had to give in and stop running. I loved to run. It was my release. I had to give it up. 'A' had beaten me..

So in June 2016 off we went to Homerton Hospital for my 2nd surgery.
I was admitted in the morning, so the wait began! Later that day I went down for the surgery and had to leave my husband to pace the streets of Hackney with worry..
Surgery was apparently very complicated, clearing lots of scar tissue, the procedure was not as simple as they expected!

I went to recovery, then later taken to the ward. My husband was there waiting for me to arrive, again I could not have done any of this without his love and constant support, he's my rock.

Within an hour the worst happened. I was given some pain medication, immediately after swallowing the tablets I was in agony. I could hardly breathe. I thought I was going to have a heart attack. The pain was that bad! I could see the pure panic on John's face, not knowing what was happening?

I was surrounded by doctors/nurses and surgeons, after they stabilised my breathing I was taken immediately down to have a scan to find out what was going on??

They discovered that I had a perforated esophagus, a risk of the surgery I had just undergone. The medication I had taken had gone through the tear in my esophagus and straight into my body which caused a bad reaction!

Then it all began.

I had to go back to surgery later that day to have a stent put into my esophagus to help seal the leak and a 'Robertson drain' in my side to monitor what amount was leaking. I was a mess and at a very very low point in my life.

John stayed up in London for a couple of days so he could be with me and to save him the commute every day, but he had to go back to work and I was in safe hands so to speak and the best place for me to be. I ended up 2 weeks in that bloody hospital, which slowly drove me crazy!

I was on a feed pipe 24/7 and couldn't drink other than suck on a sponge. I was a complete wreck.

John travelled up to London everyday after work, I don't know how he did it? He was completely knackered himself with the stress and worry and then driving all day for his job! I Worried about him all the time, his own health was suffering!

I thought I would never get out of this place, the monotony of not being able to do anything being attached to a feed tube all the time then there was the drain bag I had to carry around with me constantly.
I hated it, I hated everything in this hospital, this awful illness I was in a very dark hole, many a night after John left I would just lay there and cry myself to sleep, I just needed to get home and be in my own surroundings, my family. I couldn't take this much longer!
Finally after 2 weeks I could go home along with my stent still in place, the

feed tube still attached into my nose because of the stent I was not able to try and consume anything other than liquids and a drain from my stomach because of the perforated esophagus plus lots of antibiotics. what a relief to be going home for both of us. Although being home it sooned turned to shock and horror that very night!

Because of not eating I get enjoyment from sucking boiled sweets and I popped a Rhubarb & Custard sweet into my mouth and after sucking it for a moment I swallowed it!!! Why I don't know but the thought of it getting as far as the stent and getting stuck there scared the life out of us. We grabbed a bottle of coke and went outside pacing up and down the street drinking the coke hoping it would help it dissolve quicker!

This was pitch black about 10pm at night. When we went in, John even put one of the sweets into a glass of coke to see how long it took to dissolve. We were amazed how quick it did and then realised the panic was over.

I had to stay on a liquid diet for a further 6 weeks until the stent was ready to be removed. Also the drain again until I went back 6 weeks later. A very long 6 weeks!

The nose feed tube was a nightmare, it was embarrassing to go out. It felt as if everyone was staring, i just didn't want to go anywhere i hated it!

Because I was having issues with it they decided to take it out before the 6 weeks and let me just drink the drinks instead. What a relief, what an amazing feeling not having it I felt normal again.

I was kept under the nutritionist from the hospital and had weekly telephone consultations with her.

The day finally came I could now have my stent removed, however my drain had to stay for a further 2 weeks just to make sure when the stent was removed there was no leakage. I still remained on liquids mostly, but I was allowed to try very soft foods if possible.

It was more scary worrying about it still leaking, I was constantly checking my bag 24/7 almost to the point of being paranoid that I would end up back in that hospital if there was the slightest leak. The 2 weeks went by now at the end of august I could finally have that drain removed. What a relief to feel normal again. I could actually start wearing my clothes without worrying about the bag showing all the time.

I was able to gradually ease myself into trying food again after a few more weeks on just soft foods, then introducing other foods again [very scary]

Things started ok, trying bits and pieces of food felt like heaven to eat something again!
I don't think people realise that 'A' is a hidden autoimmune disease, from the outside everyone thinks you're ok, however if only they know what we have

to go through on a daily basis. Food features so highly in everybody's lives, birthdays, get togethers, christmas everything is food related my worst nightmare.

Someone said to me they wished they had my disease to keep their weight down! I just didn't know what to say.. If only they knew and understood our daily struggles and battles with food. I would love to just sit down and enjoy something as simple as a sandwich sit down for a meal, they have no idea whatsoever!

Life has to go on. I returned to work in October 3 months after having over 3 months off, which has had a huge financial drain on everything and added pressure on my husband to help me with my finances.

By now the worrying signs were gradually returning, day by day it was yet again getting harder to eat and keep foods down. I could only eat small bits, the feeling of fullness, the struggle trying to swallow my food down was overwhelming, why me?? I don't know many times I've questioned everything, myself, my family and my poor hubby having to go through all this with me, the ups and the downs although there are more downs than ups!

The total lack of food whilst working soon started to take its toll mentally and physically again! Later in October I had my follow up at Homerton, my surgeon/consultant believed that I may have a stricture which is caused by scarring as everything tries to heal. I had a timed Barium Swallow test scheduled for December.

My procedures had left me with a lot of pain on my left side whenever I tried to eat something it would hurt me under my ribs, something which made my 'A' harder to deal with.

Despite everything having always been a keen runner I decided to attempt going back to the gym, this made me feel good at the time but I also had no energy i couldn't re fuel my body after, so that was that no more gym. All I wanted to do was RUN!

I continued trying to eat foods whether they regurgitated or not. I was NOT going to let 'A' win, although in the end it always does. I will persevere until I really can't do it anymore!

Christmas 2016 we went out for a meal with the family and I sat there with my bottle of 'Fresubin' Meal replacement drink, how depressing..

My surgeon/consultant at Homerton decided without asking, what to me felt like he was passing me over for someone else to fix!

From Queens hospital to Homerton it just felt like they washed their hands of me because they'd run out of ideas so referred me over to the next one.

So here we went again. I was sent to see a professor at the 'Royal London Hospital' for his opinion of my Barium results etc... so in March 2017 my appointment was booked.

Everything has to carry on as normal or as normal as can be expected. Daily life for me was trying to eat, pain, regurgitate, pain then feel like crap, go to sleep hungry then wake up hungry the worst feeling ever..doing this everyday wears your body down like you could not imagine, ruins your teeth, my nails brittle, my hair would fall out easily. When I left Homerton I was prescribed by the dietician/nutritionist 'Fresubin' drinks as my food source to give me my calories and vitamins.

March came and we both had time off work to attend my first appointment with the professor who would hopefully be able to help me.

We got the train up to London and arrived only to be told the Professor wasn't there and I had to see some registrar who didn't even have all my notes or my medical records. We were fuming, outraged, we could not express our anger, nearly 4 months we had waited for this appointment. This person had absolutely NO knowledge of 'A' and tried to tell me it was all in my head and the pain on my left side was just me! Absolutely disgusted we left, oh and I mustn't forget they gave me a prescription for painkillers..

Achalasia can often be mistaken for "Bulimia" if not diagnosed properly, the symptoms of regurgitating , most GP's would diagnose Bulimia rather than investigate.

John immediately contacted 'PALS' "patient advice and liaison service" once we returned home absolutely disgusted..

1st).. The professor I supposedly had my appointment with was NOT even there or had the decency to notify us.

2nd).. Making us see a registrar and his sidekick, knowing absolutely nothing about me or my history and from what I could gather had no clue about 'Achalasia'

3rd).. Just wanted to give me painkillers and even insinuated that this illness and the eating was all in my mind.

4th).. Both of us travelling up to London especially for today and having to take time off work for this planned consultation. Not to mention the emotion of everything and being promised to be seen by the professor only to be left completely flat and deflated not having seen him! They just have no idea. Meanwhile I've been left just to carry on and no future appointment in place?

Later in the week I received a phone call directly from the professor apologising and explaining that he had to take unexpected leave, yes we all have unexpected things happen in our lives, but I Would rather he just rescheduled my appointment for a few weeks later than completely waste our time going up to London.

In April a few weeks later my appointment was rescheduled, on the same day in the morning he wanted me firstly to have a 'Manometry' test then see him after with the results. Again this is one of the worst tests you could ever experience!

This time during the test I almost had a full blown panic attack but thanks to my husband he managed to calm me down and get through it. Test done now to see the professor.

Basically the Manometry test simply confirmed how badly my 'Achalasia' was progressing.

"An esophageal motility study or esophageal manometry is a test to assess motor function of the upper esophageal sphincter, esophageal body and lower esophageal sphincter."

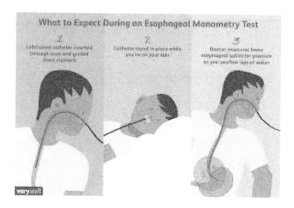

Since my surgery at Homerton all my left side had become very painful when I tried to eat anything, the professor explained to me that because of the procedures all of my nerve endings had become hyper sensitive so he prescribed 'Amitriptyline' widely used to treat neuropathic nerve damage. As for my test well he suggested that I see one of his consultants at Royal London Hospital with the view to having 'Botox' injections into the 'LES' which he believed would help me with my eating??

So here we go again! I was starting to feel like a lab rat through all these different procedures and being passed from one person to the other, it was just never ending but I had no choice. I was in their hands.

The tablets I was prescribed didn't help, they just made me feel ill, headaches and nausea so I stopped them! I had some pain management with injections and I was given a 'Tens' machine to help deal with the pain area...

So October 2017 came after months of appointments during which things had not improved. I trusted the professor's decision to go ahead and try the Botox injections, which would hopefully help me to finally get my food down easier and eat something?

On the 18th October I went into the 'Royal London Hospital' for the injections. Yet another procedure to endure.

The botox was injected via endoscopy, which I managed to do without anesthetic with only a throat spray as I did not want to have to stay there any longer than needed,had I had anesthetic I would have had to wait until it had worn off. I have still to this day have no idea how I managed to go through this 15+ minutes procedure.

Pretty hardcore considering I could feel eveything they were doing and the botox injections! The botox procedure was done and I was allowed home after an hour or so just to make sure there were no issues. I was told 24-48 hours I should be noticing differences with my food?

Wow did I !!!

Botox was the worst idea and decision made by the Professor, I wish I had researched it further, but at the time it was my only option.

Everything went wrong.. Food was even harder to get down. I was regurgitating every time I ate..

I was in immediate contact with the professor. He asked me to give things a couple of weeks to settle down and he would make a telephone consultation with me for 2 weeks time.

It was awful, yet again another failure, another disappointment, another waste of time, when will this end, when will I get some normality back into our lives? On the 30th October 2017 I had my telephone consultation with the professor.

Showing my obvious distress he requested an urgent 'Barium' swallow test and would put my case forward to the monthly meetings that are held between all of the London hospitals for next steps? What would happen now? Where does this leave me in the meantime? The Botox injections had ruined me and made everything so much worse, what can they do now?

A few weeks later I had my Barium test at the Royal London and yet again left to wait week after week for the outcome of the results.. My life was just a waiting game.

I was put on 'Fresubin' drinks by the professor to help maintain my weight and nutrition, at first they upset my stomach, I lost weight because they just went through me as I adjusted to them over the weeks so began my life on liquids! No one can know or experience what it feels like to only have a liquid diet, not being able to consume food, it restricts

EVERY part of your life every single day especially at christmas!

It plays with your head mentally, I almost started to believe that this was all in my head that I was doing it to myself, you start to question everything in your life. Christmas dinner 2017 was again a bottle of Fresubin...

The botox had completely ruined me, adding more scar tissue on top of everything else that I have done, makes me feel like a guinea pig!

For the last 3 years this has been my life with 'A' my health was not good. I suffered with fatigue on a daily basis, would this ever stop?

Later that month I had yet another panic attack, I have never in my life suffered with these only since I was diagnosed with 'A' related?? I was beginning to struggle mentally and physically, I am a strong person or so I believed but this illness was gradually wearing me down and taking every ounce of my mental and physical strength! I was so depressed..

And so the weeks went by until March 18 2018 I was informed that I would be referred to the 'UCLH' hospital in London for a private consultation with a Professor 'M' specialising in Achalasia and a Mr 'M' Upper GI surgeon.

We had our consultation in a private room, the professor had come in especially to see me as he now only worked within the private sector. It actually felt like someone really cared about my condition, understood what I was going through on a daily basis.

I was examined, my previous tests reviewed, the professor and surgeon came to the conclusion that an "OPEN CARDIOPLASTY" was my only option. They explained that because of all my previous procedures, dilations, botox and the perforated Esophagus all these cause scarring and that keyhole surgery was NOT an option as they needed to be able to deal with everything should any problems arise..

So my decision was do I or don't I go ahead?

It's a decision that although we didn't want to consider, we knew that this was the only possible option. At least the professor had given me some hope and I trusted and believed in everything that had been discussed with us both good and bad. What other choice did I have? My decision after much discussion with my husband was made to go ahead. Once confirmed I was booked in for a CT scan in April so they could have a clearer picture with what they were dealing with.

At the beginning of May we were scheduled to go and see the surgeon regarding my CT scan so off we went back up to UCLH.

Much to our disgust after waiting over 1 ½ hours Mr 'M' called us into his room to explain that there had been a terrible mistake, his secretary was supposed to contact me to cancel the appointment as he had to call an urgent cancer clinic. He could not apologise enough, yet another mess up. My husband was furious to say the least, what a complete waste of our time!

Had we been in a position financially to afford private care and treatment we would not have hesitated..

The very next morning whilst I was at work I received a phone call from Mr 'M' again apologising for yesterday. He explained that he had just liaised with the Professor and if I was in agreement they could schedule my surgery subject to pre-op results for the 13th June 18!! I was actually speechless.

I didn't know what to say? Fear and panic set in this was all quicker than I expected, although this is what I have been waiting for, for so long.. So finally things were set in place, I spoke to my Management at work, they knew of my illness and had always been supportive. My husband and I discussed the operation, the complications and the recovery. I knew my husband was scared because of the unknown and obviously this was open surgery and a complicated procedure.

So a few weeks later we were back to the UCLH for my pre-op tests and then a final consultation with Mr 'M' before my surgery, all of my results and discussions were fed back to the Professor.

For the next week or so I was stressed about the operation, I was scared and anxious. I was worrying about how my husband would cope with the worry, the travelling etc..it was a lot of pressure and worry for the both of us.

I worked on Monday, mainly to occupy my mind and keep me busy. Tuesday I was off to get myself prepared for Wednesday morning. I was so bad I thought I was going to have a panic attack... please let this work for us was all that i was thinking. I am a spiritual person and believe me I called upon everyone to get me through this and help me to cope with the recovery.
I actually slept reasonably well considering we were up very early to travel to London for my 7am check in time as i was first on the list for surgery. When I woke up I couldn't believe how calm and positive I was.
I wasn't worried, anxious or stressed about anything, I was in a very good place!

We arrived and I was asked to get into my surgical gown, socks and my paper underwear! John was understandably nervous and very anxious, although he's been here before this was completely different, **this was on a different** level to keyhole surgery..I remained very calm. Mr 'M' came to see us both before I went down to the theatre. He promised John that the moment I was out of surgery he would call him so he could stop worrying.

To the theatre I went for the prep. Firstly I was prepared for my 'Epidural' . I did expect this to be very painful but was completely pain free.

As it was being performed the Professor came in to see me and reassure me of everything that was going to be done. Again I was so very calm I was wheeled into theatre, here we go! Please let this be it... 4 to 5 hours later I woke up in the ICU. I was told I would probably be there for at least 24 hours in case of any problems. When I woke I had tubes and wires everywhere, drugged up to the eyeballs with my husband by my side as always, he must have been sick with worry pacing the streets of London waiting for me to return from the theatre.

John was allowed to stay with me, I was on Morphine for the pain so I didn't remember anything other than being prepped for surgery and speaking to the Professor before I went into surgery telling me everything would be ok. In ICU at one stage my Potassium levels went dangerously low, so they had to give me Potassium intravenously, other than that I felt surprisingly ok.

I remained in ICU until early evening and was then taken to a main ward to recover. Mr M came to see us on the ward not long after I arrived. He went through the procedure apparently they nearly abandoned the surgery because the scarring everywhere was so bad! They were very happy with what they did and with no complications, I should only be in for a week and he would come see me every day..

So here the fun began! I was on a general ward with a shift change about to happen.. Mr M had left instructions on my care and medication as he left.

As for the shift change, what a shambles, they had absolutely no clue. The nurses were all agency temps, on my ward there were 4 of us, this poor nurse had a ward of over 12 to care for! It took hours for her to get sorted.

Everyone was behind with their meds my Morphine was wearing off and extreme pain was kicking in!! I was beside myself with pain. It was horrendous I could hardly breathe, the lady in the bed next to me was calling for the nurses, John was beside himself, he demanded they called Mr M to sort this out.. I have never felt such pain!

I have every sympathy for the NHS and the nurses but maybe they should have kept me in ICU a bit longer? They were instructed by Mr M that I was to be given 'Oramorph' and 'Tramadol' as and when required. It was getting late and John headed home. It had been a long and stressful day and he needed to sleep! I could not do this without his love and support.

Although he did cause a bit of a drama one day after. I put my electric bed in the upright position and pulled a wire out the wall so John plugged it back in which would have been ok but for some reason he pressed the Red button next to it! in came running doctors, nurses with crash cart.... Ooops!

We had decided that it was best if John had a couple of days off work to start then return to work as he knew I was in the best place and he would come up to see me in the evenings after work.
I was kept medicated most of the night so I slept reasonably well considering the chaos on the wards..

The morning came and another shift changed, quite a relief to be honest after the night before!

I was now under the care of 2 wonderful nurses, very caring and checked on me regularly.

Because I was bedridden due to being all wired up and having a catheter and feeding tube fitted I had to have a bed bath, the least of my worries really!

I spoke to John in the morning to let him know that everything was ok and couldn't wait to see him later.

I was 'Nil by mouth' with only sips of water.

Mr M and his team came to see me later that morning, such a caring man he decided the feed tube could come out, checked my wound and the 20+ staples I had in what I called my shark bite, as it was shaped like a shark bite would be which went from one side of my body to the other!

He kept me on my medication and would see me again in the morning, again he said he was extremely pleased with the surgery and hoped for good results and good outcome.. John arrived and I couldn't be happier to see him, luckily I had 3 lovely ladies on my ward so there was always a good atmosphere despite everyone's predicament. Whilst John was there we had the dreaded shift change for the night again all agency temps! I again had to keep calling for my medication and reminding them, surely something should be done, there is such a shortage of nurses it's so very unfair on everybody, yet the day shift runs like clockwork without any problems!

The next couple of days the pain started to subside, the catheter was removed. Mr M was so very pleased with my wound that he decided to keep it uncovered so it would heal better. I was allowed to have liquids, yoghurts, ice cream and jelly but to take things very slowly! I could actually start to feel things go down into my stomach, what an amazing feeling..

When Mr M came to see me the next day he asked how I was feeling and how the eating was, he was so pleased he held my feet and was actually quite emotional to see good results, he said he would inform the Professor of my progress.

The weekend came and my husband stayed with me most of the day, we went for little walks, I did struggle with the pain and tightness from my wound and breathlessness.

Monday came and Mr M came to see me, told me that depending on blood tests etc.. I could go home tomorrow!! What joy I was over the moon John couldn't wait. I spent my last night on the ward and morning came. I knew it would take all day to get me discharged just from previous experience so I told John not to rush up here and just take his time. Mr M came to see me with instructions for the next few weeks.

It did take all day to get my medication, discharge letter, follow up appointment etc..

I was told only soft/liquid diet for the next few weeks and gradually introduced soft foods up until my appointment in 6 weeks time.

In the week I was in hospital I hadn't opened my bowels and I was NEVER asked if I had or if I needed a laxative? I wasn't even asked upon discharge? Unbeknown to me the awful time that I was about to experience once I returned home with serious constipation and pain like I've never experienced!!!

My husband came to collect me later in the afternoon. I was all packed and ready to leave and go home to the peace and tranquillity of my home. He had a couple of days off to make sure I was ok before he went back to work, luckily he worked locally so when he was back at work he would be able to pop home to see me or if I needed him he was just a phone call away.

Trying to get into a car and wearing a seatbelt was very painful and uncomfortable with the position and size of my wound. It was very awkward. I got into the car precariously and put a pillow on my stomach to protect me and so the journey home began.

John was so caring he drove home for the 40 mile journey so carefully and I could see how happy he was but also I knew he was so worried about me being at home for my recovery and the stress it will put him under..

I have 2 sisters and 1 brother sadly both my parents were no longer with us, my brother I hadn't seen in probably over 2 years only 1 of my sisters drove including my son but they all lived miles away which sadly left everything on John's shoulders.

I don't think I could ever put him through anything like this again!

And so began my long road to recovery and hopefully at the end a better quality of life for both of us.

We arrived home early evening a bit apprehensive about what the next few days/weeks would bring for us both?

We both slept well that night at home in bed with no noise and dosed up with painkillers. I was so glad to be home at last with my husband.

Morning came and I was very sore and tight. I dared not cough or sneeze! The wound and staples looked ok, I was due to have them removed in 2 weeks time with our local nurse.

John helped me with my first shower (heaven) clean and relaxed and still a bit weary from my medication, I was sent home with 'Tramadol' as and when required so I was trying not to have it unless I really needed it but mainly having it at night to help me sleep.

It was mainly the scar and staples that were sore and so very tight, my stomach was tender and very bloated.

As I mentioned previously I had not been checked for any bowel movement either whilst in hospital or when discharged? Therefore because of the operation and the medications I was gradually becoming more and more constipated which was about to get a whole lot worse!

Pains were gradually getting worse in my stomach from constipation and because of the staples and my wound it was hard to make myself go..

Within the next couple of days I was in agony the pain from being constipated and trying to go to the toilet was unbearable.. My stools were so hard it had become scary to even try to go to the toilet because of the pain!

John was getting worried. He tried to help me the best he could, we went to bed and I tried to relax but the pain was unbearable. John dialled 111 to get some medical advice. We had to wait for them to call back, we ended up waiting all night for a phone call back.. It was a complete waste of time.

I was over the worst by the time they called back. We managed to get a couple of hours of sleep. First thing in the morning we rang the doctors and got an emergency appointment. The doctor gave me a strong laxative solution as soon as we returned home the solution was taken. Didn't take long for things to start happening, although painful to start it was such as relief to get my bowels moving again..

The worst thing about all of this is that it could have been avoided had the hospital checked whilst I was in hospital or before I was discharged?

And so continued the recovery...
The constipation passed then pain from the operation continued for about a week. I had managed to control the pain with just paracetamol, 'Tramadol' was a last resort as it was something I didn't really want to rely on..

After a couple of days I was having some problems with my scar and the staples. I had some weeping being concerned we made a doctors appointment that morning. He was concerned about the weeping because of the possibility of infection and being such a big wound so I was put on a course of antibiotics to keep any infections at bay.

After 10 days it was time to have my staples out and let the scar heal and wow what a scar!

A few weeks went by trying to eat little bits. A few times my food was sticking in my Esophagus I was trying my best to wash it down with lots of 'Pepsi Max' something that was suggested by my previous surgeon.

6 weeks post op my acid reflux is really bad and so very uncomfortable and is at its worst at bedtime, which is giving me many sleepless nights. On top of that my scar was very painful and so very tight almost unbearable sometimes!
A week later I woke in the night having a panic attack, brought on by what I'm not sure? The acid, the pain or the worry of going up to London to see Mr M tomorrow could be any of these?

We went to London the next morning for my appointment. He was very happy with the healing and my progress, he doubled my medication for the acid reflux to try to help me. I was to continue with my foods, gradually adding different foods as I go.

10 weeks went by very slowly and it felt like forever recovering at home. The tightness I was getting from the scarring and 'Esophageal spasms' made my chest so tight I'd panic and a panic attack would start to kick in. panic attacks had become regular and luckily I was managing to control them. I was still struggling with food getting stuck and the acid reflux had become my main problem making my 'E' so sore and uncomfortable.

After 12 weeks of recovery at home I returned to work on reduced hours. My first week was exhausting physically and mentally, but I needed to get back to work and some normality back in my life. A few weeks later I started to notice a lot more issues with my eating, I was beginning to regurgitate again?? This was worrying but I was hoping it would pass. I was trying to eat smaller and even slower to see if it would help but to no avail. I hate 'A'!!!

Mr M had scheduled me for a 'Barium Swallow test' in November 2018 to investigate the problems I was beginning to have again, the regurgitating, acid reflux and the tightness. I had the test but had to wait till my appointment in December 2018 with Mr M for the results. My appointment came and the results were not good. He scheduled an 'Endoscopic' investigation to take a closer look.

So here we go again it's only been 6 months since my operation and yet still everything was going downhill! I had begun to think all this was me and all in my head? Now i know it's not! This is neverending When will I get my/our lives back?

This cruel illness affects everything in your life including those around you, it's stressful, draining and extremely emotional. Thank goodness I have the most wonderful caring and loving husband in the world. Without his love and support I doubt I would even be here today!

I had some blood tests done with my GP and my iron levels had become very low so I was prescribed Iron tablets.

Working back to normal hours especially this time of the year (December) in retail is crazy and very stressful to say the least, my body was beginning to let me down and I was struggling on a daily basis. I don't know how I was surviving?

My husband had recently completed a 'Reiki' Course , mainly his aim was to help me with my 'Achalasia' my pain and mental wellbeing. I personally would highly recommend this alternative spiritual treatment to anyone.

Reiki

Description

Reiki is a form of alternative medicine called energy healing. Reiki practitioners use a technique called palm healing or hands-on healing through which a "universal energy" is said to be transferred through the palms of the practitioner to the patient in order to encourage emotional or physical healing

We never believed Reiki would ever cure me but its healing powers help me calm down and also help me mentally deal with it. Sometimes I wake in the night and can't sleep because of the tightness and discomfort in my stomach from my scaring so John uses Reiki on me while I lay there and it helps me to deal with the pain and then go back off to sleep again. Again yet another Christmas 2018 and again NO Christmas dinner! For the last 4 years each time I had a procedure done I/we would always say "at least i'll have a Christmas dinner this year" so far I am still waiting to get tucked into one! You have no idea what it's like not being able to sit and enjoy a dinner with family or friends, without the worry and stress that if I tried to eat something it would get stuck i'd have to find a toilet to go regurgitate my food! It's such an awful disease all I do is try to eat, regurgitate and then get acid reflux, my body/scar pain the Esophageal spasms it just stops you in your tracks it's a debilitating illness..

Roll on 2019! New year new beginnings?

2019 started just as much as the last 4 years! Appointments up London , tests, consultations all over again.

February 2019 my endoscopic investigation took place, I'd begun to hate and dread hospitals, the needles, everything that revolved around them..
I was told after I came round from the procedure by Mr M's Endoscopist that my 'E' was severely inflamed , bleeding etc.. from the excessive acid reflux I was suffering with and possibly why I was struggling eating again? I was prescribed 'Sulphate liquid' to try calm the inflammation and coat my Esophagus to protect from any more harm.
I could just feel myself inside getting lower and lower physically and mentally.

I have always considered myself a strong person but this illness was gradually chipping away at me day by day. I didn't know just how much more my body could take?

After I had the operation last year, because I had started to manage bits of food, we went out and booked a holiday to Cyprus for June 19 and also a week in October 19 for my birthday to Spain to go back to a place where I spent my childhood years with my family, some very fond memories. We hadn't had a holiday abroad for over 5 years because of my illness so naturally we wanted to celebrate.

Now we are fast approaching June and naturally worry about going was beginning to set in. My husband was stressing about the food issue abroad! I couldn't take a suitcase of 'Fresubin' drinks that would be impossible.

May came round and we had an appointment up in London to see Mr M on a Saturday morning this way neither of us had to take time off from work

We discussed my results, my symptoms. Nothing had changed other than my acid reflux was better controlled.

He decided to schedule yet another 'Endoscopic investigation' for when we returned from our holiday in June.

The months just go by waiting for each appointment every test before you know it half the year has already passed and when I have my investigation next month it will have been a year since my operation! I'm no better and still waiting for an outcome? Is there a light at the end of this very long tunnel?

Despite all the worries our holiday came to Cyprus I managed the best I could and we had an amazing holiday!

I did hide a lot of how I was feeling and coping from my husband. I wanted him to enjoy this and try to stop worrying about me just for a couple of weeks at least, he deserved this break he's such a wonderful caring and loving man he's my life and i couldn't cope without him. I love him with all my heart.

We returned from our hols, back to work and still NO appointment yet arranged for my Endoscopy! I was expecting an appointment to be in place for when we returned. I waited until July, still nothing so I had to start chasing for my appointment..
My symptoms were gradually getting worse. I could hardly keep anything down, I tried to eat something on a daily basis but would then without fail have to regurgitate practically everything!

I only had a few of my Fresubin drinks left over from my previous operation so I made a request to my GP to re prescribe them. She would not unless the hospital authorised first or I went to see a Nutritionist. I ended up buying some privately to keep me going, this was becoming my only source of food.

I was on the telephone weekly to Mr M's secretary trying to get my appointment sorted so frustrating and stressful, they just don't understand what this is doing to my body, my mental state. I was becoming more and more fatigued. Finally my appointment was scheduled for the 18th September 2019!

My procedure went ahead. Sadly Mr M's Endoscopist spoke to me after, he explained and told me that during the procedure he called Mr M to attend so he could see what was found. For some reason my stomach had prolapsed into my Esophagus which basically was blocking anything going into my stomach only allowing enough room for small amounts of liquid! The consensus was that I could survive on just a liquid diet or I was looking at the possibility of an 'Esophagectomy' total removal of the Esophagus!!
Something that I never wanted to consider a horrific operation..

Overview

Esophagectomy is a surgical procedure to remove some or all of the swallowing tube between your mouth and stomach (esophagus) and then reconstruct it using part of another organ, usually the stomach. Esophagectomy is a common treatment for advanced esophageal cancer and is used occasionally for Barrett's esophagus if aggressive precancerous cells are present. An esophagectomy may also be recommended for noncancerous conditions when prior attempts to save the esophagus have failed, such as with end-stage achalasia or strictures, or after ingestion of material that damages the lining of the esophagus.

My head was all over the place! We spoke in detail about everything with the Endoscopist. He sent an urgent email to

my GP requesting an urgent prescription for Fresubin drink for the foreseeable future. My hubby was beside himself with worry about the possibility of an 'Esophagectomy' operation and all that would come with it including the recovery.

We returned home on the train contemplating our/my future and what would be? We spoke in detail what if but not too much as the thought and enormity of what could happen was very stressful for both of us.
I stayed off work the next couple of days not feeling great, very sore and to be honest I was devastated with the outcome of my investigation.
I returned to work on Monday very low and depressed. We both carried on as normal, what else could we do?
We awaited my next appointment to see Mr M to discuss my future..

I could feel myself getting pulled down into a black hole of depression, anxiety and constant fatigue. It felt like my body was just giving up!!

Weeks went by (no surprise) finally I received my appointment for November 2019..

At the beginning of October the inevitable happened.. I had been working as normal doing early and late shifts long busy days, tired and not eating! Wednesday night I just had a complete meltdown. I was hysterical, I didn't want to live anymore. I was just a hindrance to my husband and family there was just no light for me at the end of this very dark tunnel. I was screaming and shouting at my husband because I just couldn't cope with this awful illness anymore. Finally 'A' had worn me down, the strong warrior within me had been beaten and I couldn't deal with it anymore..

My body wouldn't function, I was so fatigued I could barely talk. It took hours for my hubby to calm me down. We went to bed and I said that I would be ok in the morning for work? WRONG!!!

I woke up as my husband got up for work. I couldn't open my eyes, lift my head off the pillow or even speak. I was completely done, my whole world had come crumbling down around me, I was finally defeated by 'A' I couldn't take anymore!!

John stayed off work and we made an emergency appointment with my GP. She signed me off work for at least a month, ordered blood tests and told me I needed complete rest!!

My body was shutting down, was this a cry for help? I needed to stay home to try and get the fresubin drinks down me without worrying about getting an upset stomach, now I was home it didn't matter if they did, I just needed to build myself back up as much as I could. How did I even think I could keep working week after week living on fresh air without something going wrong?

My life was a mess because of 'A' It had ruined me, taken away everything I was and changed my life forever! All I can do now is recover and get myself back on my feet again.

I rested and tried to have my fresubin drinks as much as I could although they upset my stomach every day but I needed to keep trying.

The month went by during the 2nd week I had made a coffee and placed it on my little table ready to sit down. The next thing I woke up sat down on the floor in front of the sofa, my coffee still on the table but ice cold? No idea what had happened? My sugar levels must've dropped and I passed out? I have absolutely no idea but just as well I was at home.

My appointment with Mr 'M' came and we travelled up to UCLH yet again full of anticipation. I had my list of questions ready as did my husband.

Sadly the news was not good as what had been explained previously. Mr M was himself very reluctant to try and remove the prolapse as he also explained this was not his expertees and also explained I could be opening myself up to 'Multiple' complications as he was unsure if the prolapse would contain stomach muscle? Which would cause a perforation in my stomach if there was, and until removal was attempted they would not know?

He needed to consult with some older and wiser heads (his words) about the possibility of removal done through endoscopy as he did not want to put me through unnecessary surgery. If this was not a possibility then it would mean 'Esophagectomy' was the only solution!!!

He also wanted more tests to see how

bad my 'A' and the blockage had become since the last tests. Another 'Manometry' test and a 'Timed Barium' which he wanted done before he had his meeting with the others next month. The 'others' being Professors and top consultants from other London hospitals who would specialise or had experience in my condition.

So here we go again!

It was getting harder and harder everyday for me trying to get my head around everything I've been through over the last 6 years for what? Just to keep going round and round in circles, nothing changes. I'm full of hope then all my hopes fall flat and I'm back to square one. Last year the 'Cardioplasty' was my/our big hope now I'm possibly facing even more surgery!

My first test, the 'Manometry' was arranged urgently for the 4th December 2019 and the following week my 'Timed Barium' was arranged.

Tests done I was now waiting for Mr M to call or arrange an appointment to discuss next steps.
A few weeks went by and I had heard nothing. I then started to leave message after message with his PA asking Mr M to

call me urgently to arrange an appointment/consultation with him as soon as possible.

I received a phone call from the Professor to advise me that he needs to now consult with some other professionals working within this field to decide what the best course of action was to take with me? The meeting would be just before Christmas but promised me that he would be in touch as soon as a decision was made. In the week or so waiting for the decision everything was going through my head , the enormity if it is an 'esophagectomy' the complications if they decide to try and remove the prolapse, the worry and stress was immense for us both probably more so for my husband as i know how much he worries about me..

I received my phone call, they had decided they were going to try and remove the prolapse via endoscopy! Yes there were risks involved but they seemed certain it would be minimal with a good outcome after the procedure. Professor would not be performing the procedure as this was not his speciality but he had every faith in his colleague who specialised in endoscopic procedures such as this. However I would be under his care on the ward once the procedure was completed, probably 2-3 days depending on recovery and any complications? He told me it would be done in early January. Now for the wait for the appointment..

Christmas came and went, my usual Christmas for the last 6 years (NO DINNER)!!

I've lost complete faith now in everything time ticks away and so is the quality of mine and my husband's life! I just want to be normal again, be able to go out for lunch or dinner, not worry about having to go to special occasions, the constant worry of eating. I really don't know how much more I can take of this??

January came and I still haven't heard anything! The stress in just waiting became unbearable. The constant chasing with phone call after phone call is so stressful, all this stress did NOT help my condition it makes my Achalasia worse..

Because now I had been temporarily passed to another department for the procedure I was dealing with a whole new group of people who didn't know anything about my history had never met me face to face, this was very hard for me to trust what I was being told the only person I had dealt with for the last 2+ years was the Professor who I trusted completely...

I started calling every week getting nowhere with this new department. It got to nearly the end of January and I decided to bypass the department and go directly to Mr M. No one was returning my calls, nobody cared this was getting ridiculous!!

After yet another few weeks of no communication from anybody I finally managed to get through to these people and actually got my procedure date! March 11th 2020... unbelievable, almost 2 months after I was told.. I could not be bothered to question it.

I had enough of stressing myself out about it, 11th of March it is!!
February went and my date was almost here..

I was still off work trying to build myself back up but I was very low. I could not seem to lift myself. I just needed this done and tried to move on.
My date came and off we went up to London yet again.

I was admitted and went through the procedure with the Endoscopist doing the procedure for Mr M. My husband went away to sit and wait until he was notified that I was in recovery.
I was prepped and gowned up and off I went.
Few hours later I awoke in recovery with my husband John by my side. He had been spoken to by the Endoscopist about the procedure, he had managed to remove the prolapse successfully he had

removed some other tissue which was blocking my esophagus, he had also taken biopsies for Mr M.

I was more relieved that there had been no complications although I was very sore! John stayed with me until the evening then returned home to get some rest and a good night's sleep now all the stress and worry leading up to this day was over. I knew that Mr M would not be coming to see me on the ward until the following morning. I was on liquids only until I was seen.

I had a good night's sleep and very little pain management. It was probably the best night's sleep I've ever had in all my hospital stays!

In the morning the nurses came and did the checks, later that morning Mr M came to see me explained the procedure fully and was very happy and confident with the outcome. I was told to stay on liquids for a couple of days then progress onto

very soft foods and go gradually from there.. And I was allowed home!!
My husband collected me later that afternoon with some medication and I went with everything crossed.
I was very sore for a week or so mainly having fluids. The following week I started on soft foods, still a bit sore and unfortunately I could feel things backing up once I started trying to eat softer foods, trying to stay positive. I persevered.

Sadly just after the Covid-19 Pandemic arrived and changed everything all appointments with the UCLH were cancelled and I was unable to communicate with Mr M.

Week 3 after procedure and things were no better, I tried to be positive but yet again there was no sign of improvement. Later that week Mr M's registar rang as Mr M himself was self isolating and his registrars were dealing with all of the follow ups. I explained my situation and he asked me to give it a few more weeks as there could still be swelling and may need a bit more time to settle.
We were now in May and I was struggling badly again. I had to start on my Ensure drinks and yoghurts. I tried and tried to eat food but every time i would end up regurgitating everything and I was back to square one!

I hadn't wanted to keep pestering the hospital as I was fully aware of the pressure and stress hospitals were now under with the Coronavirus Pandemic.. However I had to speak to someone about my predicament. I rang Mr M's secretary and she forwarded my message onto Mr M.

It was happening all over again in your head you start to think it's you doing it to yourself you begin to question yourself so many things go through your head I was so very low yet another procedure yet another huge disappointment for us to deal with.. I was feeling I couldn't cope with this anymore. I felt suicidal. It was awful I was going down into this never ending black hole and didn't know if I could get myself out of it??

I had to admit defeat and speak with my GP yet again because of Covid-19 it was only a telephone consultation, she prescribed some anti depressants something I had never in my life wanted to take, but I knew I had to!

I received a call later in May from Mr M's secretary giving me a telephone consultation date with him for the 2nd June 2020..

During the time leading to my appointment things were no better. It was no different than before I had my 'Cardioplasty' 2 years ago! Why me? I would not wish this awful illness on anybody it plays with your head affects you physically and emotionally in so many ways. I actually wonder what would have happened if I had never had any surgery and just left it to progress on its own.
I truly believe that all of the procedures have made my Achalasia so much worse!! If only I could go back 6 years..

2nd of June came and Mr M called and he discussed my procedure and the findings, what was done. All the biopsies came back clear which was a relief!

We discussed my condition and how things were, naturally he was very disappointed that things were back to square one. As was discussed before this procedure in March my only option now is a 'Esophagectomy' which neither of us are keen on as this is the final procedure that can be done for me. He believes that my Achalasia has reached end stage and I have zero 'Motility' in my esophagus which is causing me all these problems and would ask my GP to prescribe me some 'Prokinetics' tablets to help me with my 'Esophageal Hypomotility'.

What else can we do? He said we have nothing to lose by trying this and would ring me in a couple of months to assess my situation. Because of Covid-19 I was unable to have any investigations or tests done for at least a couple of months so this was the only option for me.

For now I have no idea what my future holds..
I am left in limbo again for at least 2 to 3 months so I'll be at the end of 2020 another year of hell and suffering, stress and worry. This sadly is the life with 'Achalasia' Many of my fellow sufferers will relate to my story some would have had a better outcome. Sadly mine hasn't! I felt the need to highlight this relatively unknown and rare illness and tell you my life for the past 6 years dealing with every situation, all of my ups and downs, the lows and the uncertainty of everything we have been and are still going through.

My struggle will go on for how long nobody knows all I can wish and pray for is a better quality of life for myself and my husband and that my overall health improves. If my only alternative is 'Esophagectomy' then so be it and I will have to put all of my trust and faith in the hands of my surgeons and pray for a good outcome.

At the end of my diaries so far another Christmas has come and gone again with NO dinner!

We are now in February 2021 the Pandemic is still with us and we are all still in lockdown..

I had a final 'Barium Meal Swallow' test in December 2020 and a follow up telephone consultation in January 2021 with Mr 'M'..

The only way forward now is an 'Esophagectomy' or face a future on liquids!
My next telephone consultation with Mr 'M' is in April 2021 to discuss this matter further..

Still hopefully heading towards that light at the end of the tunnel ...

This is my account of my own personal battle with ACHALASIA

Jean Bates

'HOW ACHALASIA CHANGED MY LIFE'

Printed in Great Britain
by Amazon